The Washington Post

Official White House photo by Annie Leibovitz

MICHELLE OBAMA
HER FIRST YEAR AS FIRST LADY

TRIUMPH
BOOKS

MICHELLE OBAMA
HER FIRST YEAR AS FIRST LADY

This book is available in quantity at special discounts for your group or organization. For further information, contact:

TRIUMPH BOOKS
542 South Dearborn Street
Suite 750
Chicago, Illinois 60605
Phone: (312) 939-3330
Fax: (312) 663-3557
www.triumphbooks.com

ISBN: 978-1-60078-311-1
Printed in U.S.A.

Produced by *The Washington Post*
Book Editor: Mary Hadar
Photo Editors: Michel du Cille, Bonnie Jo Mount
Art Directors: Justin Ferrell, Jon Wile
Assistant Editor: Steve Reiss
Copy Editor: Mike Stuntz

Previous page photo by Marvin Joseph

Contents

BRAVO
**The first lady applauds Mel Brooks, far left, Bruce Springsteen
and the other honorees at the Kennedy Center Honors.**

1

A New Era

Michelle Obama's ascension to first ladyhood changed
the Washington culture. Here was a child of a different background
who had different ideas about what the office should be.

Photo by John McDonnell

So much started to change once Michelle Obama became first lady on Jan. 20, 2009. The sight of this African American woman standing on the Capitol steps registered like a series of rolling tremors, uprooting cultural assumptions and cliches about what it means to be a black woman, about the nature of the black family, about femininity, beauty and even social status. She did not erase generations of damaging stereotypes as she held Lincoln's Bible in her gloved hands while her husband took the presidential oath of office. But she forced many of us to reconsider what we had assumed to be true.

Michelle Obama came to her position by default. Unlike the president, she did not campaign to be first lady. She had stumped for his victory, not her own. Voters dissected her background, mused about her temperament and argued over the depths of her patriotism. But still, we didn't really choose her. Would she be the right person for such an imprecisely defined role? What would she do in her first year? What would she seek to accomplish?

The cultural conversation about her — Michelle, Mrs. O, first lady Michelle — began with surprising intimacy. It started with her clothes, which didn't jibe with the traditions of the modern first lady. She didn't wear trim suits that hid her figure. At times, it even seemed as though she were flaunting her shape. And hers was not the physique of a delicate flower or a matron. Instead, it was athletic, muscular and soared almost six feet in height.

Her figure was at odds with the kind of beauty the fashion industry and Hollywood had long held up as the standard. Michelle was not blonde, fine-boned, narrow-hipped or white. She not only defied the mainstream definition of beauty, she did it with profound confidence and ease. And she did it on the

MIXING IT UP

Tenth- and 11th-grade students and their White House partners at a November mentoring event.

Photo by Marvin Joseph

INTRODUCING BO: The Obamas take first pup Bo, a Portuguese water dog, for a stroll on the White House lawn.

world stage. Our gal boarding Air Force One, sitting in the first lady's box, greeting world leaders and posing for the cover of Vogue was a brown-skinned black girl from a working-class, Chicago family, all grown up.

Michelle's figure also matched popular culture's archetype of the black female form. And while it seemed — and still seems — wholly inappropriate to engage in a public discourse about the anatomy of a first lady, it was discussed with great pride in private conversations within the black community

and on freewheeling blogs. At other times, a minority of the public chatter would turn ugly, rife with a racism that seemed to come straight out of pre-Civil War America.

But it was hard to deny her accomplishments. Her résumé spoke of intelligence and achievement. She was a bootstrapper, an American overachiever. The wide-eyed awe was at times so extreme it seemed that people had forgotten that all those African American women who graduate from college have to go somewhere and do something. Did people

Photo by Bill O'Leary

assume such women automatically disappeared into a middle management bureaucracy?

She embodied a formidable combination: brains and beauty. America has strained to imagine such a character, at least one wrapped in brown skin. Women like Michelle are mostly invisible in the mainstream television and film world. They exist only on the fringes, playing to niche audiences that already know of their existence. Michelle loudly announced the presence of women like herself. She was Clair Huxtable writ large — the antithesis

of the angry black woman. That fire-breathing stereotype comes out of the black power '60s, a time of militancy and political strife. And ever since, African American women have struggled to shed that image, because while it honors their strength, it denies their femininity and ignores their vulnerability. During the campaign, Michelle had been depicted as Angela Davis on an ironic New Yorker magazine cover. Soon after the inauguration, she was referred to as "Stokely Carmichael in a designer dress."

To avoid having that cliche dog her for the next four years, the new first lady couldn't get angry. She couldn't come across as too adamant or too demanding. Women, in general, know how easy it is to be classified as shrill, or worse, simply because they speak with force and bluntness. During her first year in the White House, Michelle trod lightly and made sure to always smile and wave.

As she began to travel the world — from Russia to Denmark to Ghana — she showed foreigners a different part of black American culture, one that did not involve music videos, long-suffering welfare mothers or neck-snapping beleaguered girlfriends. In front of foreign audiences, she was a curiosity, an affirmation of liberal ideology and proof that anything is possible in America.

Her first state dinner seemed an inordinately treacherous test. In November, the Obamas welcomed India's prime minister to the White House. People not only wondered whether bilateral relations would be improved thanks to this diplomatic breaking-of-bread, they breathlessly waited to see what kind of hostess the first lady would be. How would she blend the administration's mantras of change and openness with the unavoidable demands of international protocol and tradition?

Michelle decided to move the dinner from the State Dining Room to a pavilion constructed on the South Lawn. The shift allowed her to invite nearly 400 guests rather than the usual 130 or so. The evening turned out to be an elegant and glamorous affair with romantic chandeliers wrapped in ivy, white votives floating in glass vases, a vegetarian menu prepared by guest chef Marcus Samuelsson and entertainment by the National Symphony Orchestra, "Slumdog Millionaire" composer A.R. Rahman and pop singer Jennifer Hudson.

EN ROUTE
The first couple on their way to Europe in the spring, starting with a short hop on Marine One.

Photo by Bill O'Leary

It was a beautiful night, but it was overshadowed by an embarrassing and dangerous security breach. A Virginia couple managed to waltz into the White House uninvited. The Secret Service apologized; the social secretary's office was swallowed up in controversy. And the first lady's silver sequined, one-of-a-kind gown by Indian-born designer Naeem Khan faded into a footnote.

In early December, in the shadow of the state dinner controversy, Michelle previewed the White House Christmas decorations. It was a sober presentation, a surprisingly joyless few minutes in front of assembled media and volunteers. For an administration that had come in waving a flag of change and for a first lady with a glamorous streak, Christmas was wholly traditional with only subtle hints of whimsy. The theme for her first Christmas in Washington was "Reflect, Rejoice and Renew." Instead of a glittering and lush holiday extravaganza, she had filled the rooms with understated trees and garlands, wreaths and a Nativity. Rather than commissioning a series of new decorations, she recycled 800 ornaments from previous administrations, sending the baubles out to local community groups and asking volunteers to re-imagine them in honor of their favorite local landmarks.

It had been a difficult year for the country: two wars, a recession and a dismal job market. Perhaps what people needed was reassurance that everything was going to be okay. The future isn't going to look like the past. But the best of the past would not be lost.

Much of the first lady's job is bound up in symbolism and her time taken up with hosting duties. The fact that aesthetic decisions fall to her is an anachronism in this age. And many assumed that Michelle, with her intellectual heft and work experience, would chafe at such homey concerns. So they were stunned when she announced that her primary role in the White House would be as mom in chief. They weren't asking Michelle to break a glass ceiling; instead, they wanted her to break out of the gilded cage that has trapped so many first ladies. All too often, these accomplished, educated women were akin to decorative birds — seen but not heard, with no real role other than to provide an air of gentility in the hard-bitten world of politics, to coo words of comfort and encouragement to the president, to keep his moral compass aligned. In her spare time, this modern caricature was expected to look pretty and to update the White House china collection — but stir no controversy over how much all those place settings would cost. Was Michelle really planning to settle onto her perch at 1600 Pennsylvania Ave. and proceed to do little more than quietly preen?

As it would turn out, being mom in chief entailed a broader agenda than many assumed. She focused on nutrition, healthy diets and childhood obesity. She organized the planting of the White House Kitchen Garden, a vegetable patch that would do much to define her first year. She announced a mentoring program for high school girls from the Washington metropolitan area who would be given guidance by top women working in the Obama administration. And she helped make the case for health care reform by visiting community health centers, hosting receptions for senior women and breast cancer survivors.

In her first 365 days, though, Michelle struggled to make her voice heard in a way that would allow her to break free of her celebrity aura and to be seen as more than merely "the first." Her uniqueness fueled constant questioning about how we would all be different because of the path that she was walking.

As might have been predicted, Michelle and the country have only begun to change in the course of a year. But we can no longer assume that the status quo is how things will always be.

SOUTH LAWN LANDING
After a winter weekend in Chicago, Michelle steps from Marine One to a salute.

Photo by John McDonnell

FOR THE CHILDREN!

In April Michelle invited congressional spouses and children to help assemble bags of food for students who depend on the Capital Area Food Bank to eat.

Photo by Bill O'Leary

GO, BRO
Michelle reacts to a close play in a men's basketball game at George Washington University. The team was playing Oregon State, which is coached by her brother, Craig Robinson. Barack and Michelle's mother are less demonstrative.

Photo by John McDonnell

AND THEN THERE WAS LIGHT

Before an audience of nearly 10,000, the first family — the president, Malia, Sasha and Michelle — presses the button to illuminate the National Christmas Tree on the Ellipse.

Photo by Ricky Carioti

The Symbol

From the start, Michelle's every move was scrutinized
for hidden meaning, but her staff tried to guard
the real woman inside the bubble — with mixed results.

Photo by Marvin Joseph

T he rise of Michelle Obama as an icon — of fashion, black womanhood, working motherhood and middle-class success — occurred over the course of almost three years, spanning a marathon presidential campaign and a year in the White House as first lady. Enthusiastic supporters, with their eyes cast toward the distant horizon of history, propelled her onto a pedestal that would surely have given the average person vertigo. Michelle was cast as Jackie Kennedy, Sojourner Truth, Hillary Clinton and a Horatio Alger character, all zipped into a Talbots sun dress.

Michelle had slipped into that rarefied world in which normal human behavior is perceived as extraordinary. Concern for her children suddenly exemplified saintly devotion, and attempts to make the White House a more welcoming and open home were seen by some as wreaking havoc with the Social Register.

For much of her first year, critics spoke out at their peril. An army of bloggers, mainstream writers and pundits railed against any criticism of the first lady — whether it was nuanced and constructive or angry and petty; her fan base made little distinction. They declared an Internet Code Red at the slightest hint of a threat, as if she needed to be protected like the last snow leopard. Fans wrapped her in a protective cocoon, a place where human failings are denied, bad hair days don't exist and dimwitted attacks can't simply be ignored.

It may be that no matter what she does during her tenure as first lady, nothing will surpass the cultural resonance of her mere presence. Michelle Obama is Clair Huxtable made real. She is undeniable evidence of what accomplished, stylish black women

HOSTESS

The first state dinner, given for Indian Prime Minister Manmohan Singh in November, was an iconic moment for the first lady.

Photo by Marvin Joseph

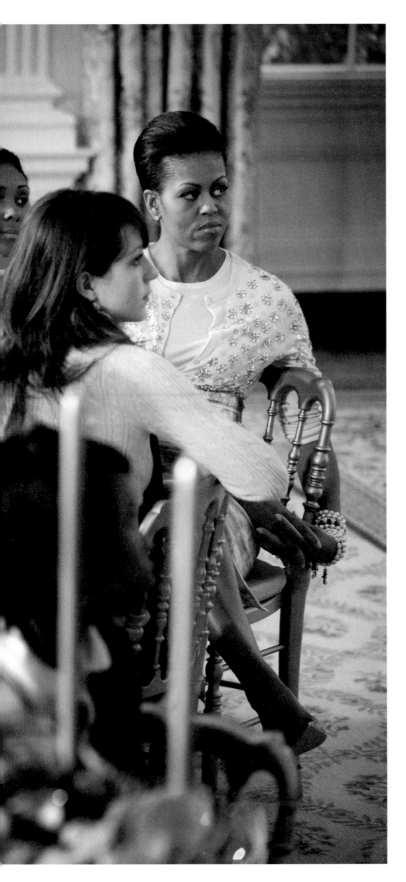

and their functional black families had known for so long. We exist. Michelle is extraordinary. But she is not exceptional. She represents a community larger than herself — a world of middle-class success and achievement. A black community free of pathology and dysfunction. A place of normalcy that seemed beyond the capacity of Hollywood, Seventh Avenue and even Madison Avenue to truly imagine. And it is thrilled to be brought out of the shadows.

Michelle Obama's importance as a symbol doesn't diminish her accomplishments, nor does it make light of her struggles. The White House is a strange cultural focal point in which details are magnified, sentences are parsed and the best intentions become fodder for inside-the-Beltway squabbling.

Her place in history is secure. But what has she actually done? Is she an agent of change or merely an inspirational photo op? By spring 2009, she had begun to make good on her early pledge to broaden the range of guests welcomed into the White House. In her first year, 1600 Pennsylvania Ave. was a vibrant place that celebrated cultural and artistic curiosity — both old guard and new. Poets jammed in the East Room, with James Earl Jones performing a soliloquy from "Othello" and a young Chicagoan reciting a poem of personal revelation to a hip-hop beat. Students, rich and poor, participated in tutorials taught by the veterans and the prodigies of jazz, country, Latin and classical music. On her watch, the traditional Easter Egg Roll went high-tech and online so that kids across the country — or more precisely, their parents — had a chance to nab a ticket for a date with the national Easter Bunny.

Along the way, there were, of course, missteps. Her often-impassioned remarks fell on deaf

HISTORY LESSON
Before the state dinner, Michelle joins the young women of the White House Leadership and Mentoring Program for a presentation on the protocol of state visits.

Photo by Marvin Joseph

ears. Fascination with her attire sometimes overshadowed interest in her platform. In celebration of Saint Patrick's Day, Michelle tinted the water in the White House fountain green — a move that arguably crossed the line from whimsical into kitsch. She set a goal of visiting every major government agency to thank longtime federal employees for their service. She had bureaucrats cheering and unflappable locals swooning. But after a few months, the gratitude visits became interchangeable and felt perfunctory. They featured the same script and the same laugh lines — "many of you have been doing this work for longer than I've been alive!" she'd say.

She attempted to put her background in community-based health care to use. Before coming to Washington, she'd been an executive at the University of Chicago Medical Center and she had helped to build a mutually beneficial relationship between the elite hospital and its working-class neighbors. Yet her remarks on behalf of health care reform rarely reached beyond the choir already convinced of the urgency of the issue. She hosted afternoon gatherings in the White House gardens and grand salons to highlight the unique medical needs of women. She described the hurdles women faced after they had survived breast cancer and then found that insurance companies treated their long-gone disease as a disqualifying pre-existing condition. She focused on the particular health care needs of older women. She traveled the Washington region cutting ribbons at community health care centers and extolled the virtues of these neighborhood medical providers. But for all her knowledge and her expressed urgency, no matter that she characterized health care as an issue both of civil rights and gender equity, she seemed to be making her declarations into a soundproofed room. They simply did not reverberate much beyond each day's event. They were so carefully calibrated not to stir controversy — avoiding topics like abortion and benefits for

same-sex couples — that they stirred almost nothing at all.

Despite the historic nature of her position, Michelle, like every other modern first lady, struggled in her initial 12 months to find her voice, define her role, put her stamp on White House culture and avoid doing her husband's administration any harm.

No event characterized that dilemma more than the G-20 summit in Pittsburgh, when she served as

hostess for the spouses program. During the two-day September gathering, she led the wives — the husbands of world leaders did not participate in the all-girls club — to philanthropist Teresa Heinz Kerry's Rosemont Farm to underscore her interest in sustainable farming. The women toured the Andy Warhol Museum. Students from a local performing arts school entertained them. The ladies lunched and dined and chatted. And they posed for photographs.

The days' events were devoid of news and heavy

MUSICAL MOMENT
The first lady introduces performers at a Classical Music Student Workshop, part of her effort to expand the range of guests welcomed into the White House.

Photo by Marvin Joseph

on uplift. In fact, it would be an exaggeration even to say the activities spotlighted the first lady's personality. No, no, no. Her staff was quite specific in describing the schedule as a reflection of her interests. "Personality" might imply that her VIP tour of Pittsburgh was too focused on the first lady — too much about Michelle and not enough about the Obama administration.

Being a cultural icon is not for the faint of heart or the introvert. How unnerving it must be to know that the menu at your first state dinner, for India, was parsed by everyone from farming trade groups to foreign policy analysts. That what you omit from your remarks about health care is more important than what you say. Can an African American icon have a cranky day in public without being dubbed an angry black woman? Michelle Obama spent her first year so relentlessly avoiding controversy, so watchful of any missteps, that she put herself in danger of being solely a symbol — and not a woman. By the time Thanksgiving rolled around, her press secretary was even denying that the first lady had a cold. Icons, it seems, do not get congested.

One wished that some close friend had stepped forward and done for the first lady what she pointedly tried to do for her husband early on in the campaign, which was to humanize him, to diminish expectations by publicly sharing details like he snores or he's stinky in the morning. The first lady needed a killjoy to tell her over-exuberant fans that, perhaps, she doesn't always remember to put away the milk. That she skips the weekly pedicures. Remind the media that everything isn't partisan, political or symbolic. Give the woman a break; debunk the mythology. Or at least try.

MULTICULTI

For International Women's Day, Michelle is joined by Secretary of State Hillary Clinton and honorees from Uzbekistan, Russia, Afghanistan, Guatemala, Iraq, Malaysia and Niger.

Photo by Richard A. Lipski

PULLING STRINGS
Performers at the White House classical music workshop concert include, from left, cellist Alisa Weilerstein, guitarist Sharon Isbin, Sujari Britt, 8, and Jason Yoder, 16.

66 *The arts are not just a nice thing to have or to do if there is free time or if one can afford it. Rather, paintings and poetry, music and fashion, design and dialogue, they all define who we are as a people and provide an account of our history for the next generation.*"

Michelle Obama,
at New York's Metropolitan
Museum of Art

Photos by Marvin Joseph

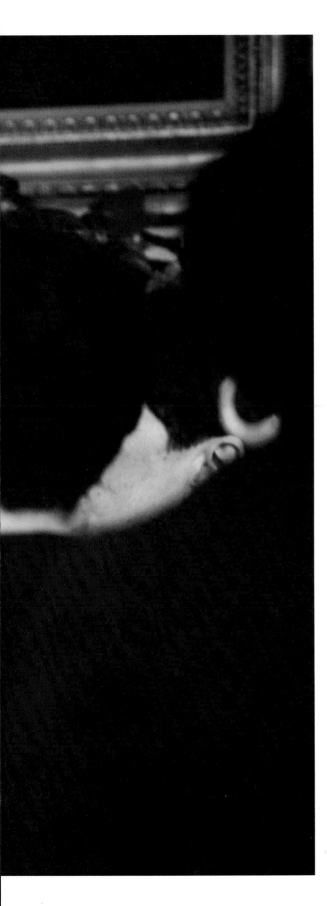

BIG HUG

A student gets a typically enthusiastic welcome from the first lady. Left, Michelle chats with singer Alicia Keys, who joined a group of women Michelle assembled to visit local schools.

Above photo by Marvin Joseph, left by Bill O'Leary

KID TIME: Michelle talks to children of Executive Office employees on Take Your Child to Work Day.

Photo by Bill O'Leary

ROLL 'EM!

Revving up the crowd at the Easter Egg Roll on the South Lawn of the White House.

Photos by Bill O'Leary

OLÉ!

With students at a charter school in Washington celebrating Cinco de Mayo.

Photo by Lois Raimondo

TWO FACETS OF THE JOB

**Mentor in the daytime, as
Lincoln looks on, and hostess
in the evening.**

*Above photo by Bill O'Leary,
left by Marvin Joseph*

66 *For the Obama family, Christmas and the new year has always been a time to reflect on our many blessings, to rejoice in the pleasure of spending time with our family and our friends, and to renew our commitment to one another and to the causes that we believe in. And I wanted to continue that part of the tradition during our first holiday season here at the White House.*"

Michelle Obama,
at the unveiling of the
White House decorations

NEW HOME FOR THE HOLIDAYS
Michelle accepts the official White House Christmas tree at the North Portico of the White House with her daughters. The 18½-foot Douglas fir arrived on the traditional horse-drawn carriage from the Shepherdstown, W.Va., farm of Gloria Sundback, grinning at right.

Photo by Marvin Joseph

GOOD ENOUGH TO EAT

The first lady thanks volunteers who helped ready the White House for Christmas. Left, the gingerbread White House constructed by pastry chef Bill Yosses and his team features the Obamas' dog Bo at the front door.

Photos by Marvin Joseph

ALL DRESSED UP
The finished tree and some of its ornaments, which were sent out to communities across the country to be decorated with local themes and returned.

Photos by Marvin Joseph

RED CHRISTMAS

Right, two Fraser firs in gilded Versailles boxes are accented with cranberries and red ribbons to make the Red Room even more rosy. Above, the State Dining Room, top, and the East Room.

Photos by Marvin Joseph

3

Her Style

In her clothing as well as her attitude,
Michelle brought an eclectic touch to the White House.
Despite an occasional misfire, she sent a message
of fashion confidence to the American people.

Photo by Marvin Joseph

F ew first ladies have caused so much breathless anticipation of their Inauguration Day wardrobes as Michelle Obama. As soon as she stepped onto the national stage as the candidate's wife, she was elevated to a fashion star by Seventh Avenue and the media, one whose tastes ran from high-end designers to the mass marketer H&M. Adding to the public's fascination with her style, Michelle, at nearly 5 feet 11 inches, had the impressive height of a runway model but the figure of a real woman — a size 12 according to one fashion publicist. She even publicly admitted to taking delight in looking "pretty."

For the historic moment when she became this country's first African American first lady, Michelle chose a lemon-grass yellow, lace sheath with a matching coat by the Cuban-born designer Isabel Toledo. The dress followed her curves — paying special attention to her full hips — and announced that the era of first lady-as-rectangle had ended. The ensemble signaled a shift in what first ladies could be on the national stage. They could boldly embrace color and reveal their power, their femininity and their shape.

For her inaugural gown, she chose another young New York-based designer, Jason Wu. His custom-made creation, in flowing ivory silk chiffon with a single strap, was embroidered with silver thread and adorned with Swarovski crystal rhinestones. It was the most revealing gown that a first lady had donned for an inauguration since Nancy Reagan wore a James Galanos dress to usher in Ronald Reagan's first term. Wu's creation bared Michelle's buff arms and toned shoulders and brought the first lady into the modern world, in which glamour is defined by Hollywood's red carpet

FIRST DAY

At the oath-taking, Michelle holds the Bible while wearing a yellow lace outfit by Isabel Toledo.

Photo by Jonathan Newton

rather than the Main Line in Philadelphia.

Her confidence on Inauguration Day gave no hint of the ambivalence she felt about the public's obsession with her style. She enjoys fashion but does not want to be remembered as "The First Lady Who Dressed Well." Still, during her freshman year in the White House, with the help of friend Ikram Goldman, a Chicago retailer, Michelle crafted the liveliest, most international, idiosyncratic and progressive public wardrobe of any modern first lady. She embraced adventurous young American designers such as Kate and Laura Mulleavy of Rodarte, who have found inspiration in such outré places as Japanese horror films. She wore the sisters' burnt-orange cocktail dress in Copenhagen when she lobbied — unsuccessfully, it would turn out — the International Olympic Committee, on behalf of her Chicago hometown, for the 2016 games. The work of Paris-based iconoclast Azzedine Alaia figured prominently in her wardrobe, including his biker-inspired wide leather belt, which she wore regularly on the world stage. She even made room for fashion's avant-garde, including Japanese designer Junya Watanabe, whose asymmetrical, collage cardigan caused a stir — Why are her seams showing? — on a trip to London.

Michelle assembled an international state wardrobe, one that dismissed the nationalistic notion that America's first lady should wear only American designers on public occasions. Instead, her style reflected the changing nature of the world, in which economies and cultures are interconnected.

She also continued to incorporate less-expensive brands, particularly J. Crew, Liz Claiborne and Talbots, into her public wardrobe. Those mall brands marked her as a kindred spirit to everyday women. In a political universe in which presidents now measure their "regular guy" bona fides by whether voters would want to have a beer with them, Michelle provided an equally banal measure for first ladies: Would women want to

go shopping with her? The more modest brands also acknowledged the harsh economic times that greeted the Obamas when they arrived in Washington. There was no denying the recession that had overwhelmed the country. Americans didn't want to see the first lady dressed in hand-me-downs, but neither did they want her outfitted in apparel that cost more than the cars

they could no longer afford.

Michelle Obama has often been compared to Jacqueline Kennedy, the last first lady who so thoroughly embraced style as a form of crowd-pleasing communication rather than merely embellishment. Both women used clothes to help set a tone for their husbands' administrations. Jackie capitalized on the fairy-tale aura that hovered over

At Norfolk Naval Base, Michelle welcomed sailors home in a (gasp!) sleeveless dress.

Photo by Marvin Joseph

the young president and his family. Michelle used her wardrobe to underscore the thread of change that is a theme of her husband's administration.

Her official White House portrait was a superb example of her fashion fluency. She wore a simple black Michael Kors sheath with a double strand of chunky pearls. The image was deceptively simple, yet eloquent. The dress was made of jersey. It's the quintessential modern fabric, desired because of its sensual drape, the manner in which it clings tastefully to the body and resistance to wrinkling. It's both indulgent and efficient.

The dress was cut with a racer back. The silhouette is common in swimsuits, running jerseys and other athletic wear. The shape emerged from the world of fitness and it underscores the ways in which women have become so much more aware of and confident in their physicality.

The most notable aspect of Michelle's dress, however, was that it was sleeveless. In the narrowly defined sartorial world of first ladies, this means something other than that perhaps it was warm on the day the photograph was taken. Generally, the women who have occupied the White House have been loath to appear sleeveless in public, as if the upper arms were erogenous zones never to be revealed in mixed company. It's also true that a significant number of women, beginning as early as their 30s, demur from revealing their arms out of self-consciousness that theirs are not as sinewy as the limbs of a yoga master. While Michelle doesn't look as though she spends half her day with a personal trainer, she looks fit and she's got the arms to prove it. That sleeveless dress announced her strength. Read that as literal or metaphorical.

In her stance, she displays the body language

SPOT OF SUNSHINE
For the National Design Awards, Michelle chose a bright yellow suit that was both form-fitting and attention-getting.

Photo by Marvin Joseph

of an athlete. She isn't sitting sedately in a gilded chair or standing demurely with her arms hanging limply at her side or with her hands clasped neatly in front. Instead, she stands with one hand resting lightly on a piece of furniture, as if she paused for the photograph mid-stride. Michelle Obama is a post-Title IX political spouse. One who offered her husband a hug and a kiss but also a fist bump of team spirit.

In her first year, she both excelled and misfired on the fashion stage. There were glamorous black dresses for date night with the president and an emerald green cocktail dress when Stevie Wonder was honored with the Gershwin Prize at the White House. There were myriad cardigans, including one she wore when she met Queen Elizabeth II at Buckingham Palace that some critics deemed too casual for such an auspicious occasion. And she favored a handful of signature belts cinched eccentrically high on her torso, giving every ensemble an Empire waist and often making her look as though her legs were directly connected to her chest.

She also wore shorts — infamous and memorable for all the wrong reasons. They weren't walking shorts or pedal pushers. They were thigh-skimming athletic shorts. She had them on when she toured the rim of the Grand Canyon while on vacation with her family.

The shorts were, in a word, jarring. Fashion can be an indispensable tool for delivering a message about approachability and empathy. But when the first couple disembarked from Air Force One, military personnel stood at attention, shutters clicked and minions scurried. Ultimately, the first lady can't be — nor should she be — just like everyone else. Hers is a life of responsibilities and privileges. She gets the fancy jet. She has to dress for the ride.

Avoiding the appearance of queenly behavior — and ostentatious style — has been politically wise for Michelle Obama. But on that summer day,

CRAZY FOR CARDIGANS
Hosting young women from the White House Leadership and Mentoring Program and, at right, visiting the Office of Personnel Management.

Above photo by Marvin Joseph, right by Bill O'Leary

she did herself no favors. By trying so hard to be average she wound up looking common.

Despite those misjudgments, however, Michelle's freshman year wardrobe was refreshingly eclectic and personal. Rarely did she wear the stately suits that most recent first ladies have favored. She had signatures, but she did not have a uniform. Each ensemble seemed created wholly out of her imagination, intended to please rather than appease. The guiding principle was contemporary style: How does a modern woman dress?

CONFIDENTLY CASUAL
**Top, a visit to an elementary school;
above and at right, welcoming students
to work on the Kitchen Garden.**

Photos by Marvin Joseph

BASIC BLACK

From left, the official White House photographic portrait, featuring a Michael Kors sheath that shows off Michelle's healthy shoulders; a black dinner dress for her "date night" with the president in New York; a jacket and boots on her return from a weekend in Chicago.

Above left by J. Scott Applewhite of Associated Press, right by Bill O'Leary

INFORMAL TO A FAULT?

Disembarking from Air Force One to tour the rim of the Grand Canyon, the first lady is dressed like her preteen daughter, an image jarringly at odds with the family's military escort.

Photo by Associated Press

PLAYING HOSTESS

Michelle wore bright orange at the welcoming ceremony for the prime minister of India and, left, a strapless, glamorous gown by Indian-born designer Naeem Khan for the state dinner.

Above photo by Bill O'Leary, left by Marvin Joseph

MICHELLE OBAMA
HER FIRST YEAR AS FIRST LADY

LOOK AT HER

It was the most revealing gown that a first lady had donned for an inauguration since Nancy Reagan wore a James Galanos dress to usher in Ronald Reagan's first term. It brought the first lady into the modern world, in which glamour is defined by Hollywood's red carpet rather than Philadelphia's Main Line.

Photo by Richard A. Lipski

4

The Nurturer

Michelle quickly showed that her "mom in chief" persona
extended beyond her own children to the world at large.

Photo by Bill O'Leary

In the months before the inauguration, Michelle Obama described her upcoming job as "mom in chief," implying she would direct most of her energy at ensuring that daughters Sasha and Malia settled happily into their new life in the White House, with a full complement of soccer games, sleepovers and Miley Cyrus concerts.

Activist feminists, political rabble-rousers and media busybodies read that description as a gentle letdown — that this Harvard-trained lawyer, former city government bureaucrat and hospital executive would not be transforming her East Wing office into an adjunct of the West. She would not try to influence policy. She would not be controversial. She would not be Hillary Clinton. If anything, she would be more like Laura Bush.

But it turns out that Michelle's definition of "mom in chief" was broader, more complicated and more nuanced than most had assumed. In her first year, she sketched out a job description that had nurturing at its core. She would turn parental mantras such as eat-your-vegetables and go-out-and-play into policy initiatives on healthy eating and exercise. At her behest, mentoring young Washington-area students became part of the daily responsibilities of senior White House staff. Michelle would offer tough love to students in some of the capital's most underserved neighborhoods, empathizing with their modest circumstances but still putting the responsibility for success in their hands.

She began simply enough with the White House Kitchen Garden. It was started with the help of fifth graders from the District's Bancroft Elementary School, in April 2009. It was a symbolic gesture and one that made for pleasant, controversy-free

PROJECT HOOP
At the healthy kids fair on the South Lawn in October, what goes around comes around, 142 times.

Official White House photo by Samantha Appleton

photographs. Sweet-faced children helped the first lady — dressed in a black tunic and matching knee-high boots — till a patch of earth on the South Lawn. It was hard to argue against children and organic vegetables — although some people complained that after the cameras disappeared the first lady's staff was doing most of the weeding and watering.

In many ways, the images of the first lady harvesting sweet potatoes and pushing a wheelbarrow heaped with lettuce replaced a host of stereotypes that had dogged her with one of her own choosing. Instead of the aggrieved minority finding fault with America, she appeared as a Whole Foods version of Mother Earth. She shed the hyper-glamorous image that had been foisted upon her by

the fashion industry and that she had encouraged by posing for a host of glossy magazine covers. She may not have had dirt under her manicured fingernails, but she at least got a little mud on her knees.

The abundance that the garden produced — more than 740 pounds of vegetables and herbs — has been used to feed everyone from the first family

REVERENCE AND READING
At right, the family attends Easter service at St. John's Episcopal Church, where every president since James Madison has worshiped at least once. Above, Michelle leads after-school lessons for third graders.

Right photo by Katherine Frey, top by Bill O'Leary

and White House guests to the homeless who come to the meals program at the District's Miriam's Kitchen for sustenance. And the garden has resonated internationally, with folks from London to Moscow curious about how it was created, how the plants are faring and the impact it might have on broader agricultural objectives such as sustainable farming and organic production.

The garden was the beginning of the first lady's wide-ranging program to curb childhood obesity, to change the unhealthy eating habits of a nation and to connect all of that to the notion that universal health care is the next step in the civil rights movement. It would lead to health fairs, including one in which Michelle would spin a hula hoop around her waist for 142 revolutions. There would be a White House Halloween party at which the first lady — dressed as a kitty cat — handed out dried fruit as well as cookies and M&M's. And she would join forces with Big Bird of "Sesame Street" to take the cause of good nutrition straight to kids in their homes.

The garden would also further a dialogue about personal responsibility that had begun a month earlier in Washington and which Michelle later took on the road to Denver. In March, for Women's History Month, she gathered 21 accomplished female actors, scientists, entrepreneurs and athletes at the White House and had them fan out to local schools to talk to students about how they could achieve beyond their wildest dreams. Michelle visited Anacostia High School, in one of the District's poorest neighborhoods, where she shared her life story with students. She told them that she was not exceptional. She hadn't started with any

FAMILY GETAWAY

Ready to board Marine One for a weekend trip to Chicago, with Michelle's mother leading the way. Marian Robinson made the move to Washington to help with child care.

Photo by Gerald Martineau

high-powered connections. No secret formulas for success.

"We didn't have a lot of money. I lived in the same house my mother lives in now. . . . I went to public schools," she said. "The fact is, I had somebody around me who helped me understand hard work. I had parents who told me, 'Don't worry about what other people say about you.' I worked really hard. I did focus on school. I wanted an A. I wanted to be smart. Kids would say: 'You talk funny.' 'You talk like a white girl.' I didn't know what that meant."

Her comments resonated much farther than that single classroom. They would be mentioned again in June by Jasmine Williams when the first lady delivered the graduation address at Washington Mathematics Science Technology school, the public charter high school where Williams was a senior.

Williams had pleaded with Michelle to attend her commencement exercises. And in her letter, Williams referred to her as "first lady Michelle" — a phrase that was a mixture of respect and informality. Williams and the school's mostly African American and Latino students said they found a kinship in the stories the first lady had repeated about being a black girl from a working-class family in Chicago who wasn't expected to achieve a fraction of what she has.

For Williams, the most memorable moment since Michelle became first lady was when she spoke to those students in Anacostia. "She told them how a lot of people told her she spoke like a white girl." Williams says she, too, refuses to buy into the idea that black students are incapable of eloquence, of debate-quality erudition, of confident personal expression.

As Williams and the other graduating seniors stepped on stage, one by one, to receive their diploma, the first lady, smiling brightly, embraced each student for a commemorative photograph that would no doubt find its way onto a mantel or a boast wall. As one young woman paused to have her picture taken, she took the opportunity to throw her

Photo by Bill O'Leary

hand up with fingers raised in a sign of victory or peace or just plain tough-girl cool. The student was smirking rather than smiling. Her head was tossed back and her torso tilted to the side in a manner that was all bravado and superiority.

The first lady seemed to recognize the damage all that adolescent bluster could do. So with her left arm still loosely encircling the student's shoulders, she used her right hand to gently pull the girl's hand down, drawing it in toward the child's heart, all the while hugging her even tighter. In a matter of seconds, the girl's body language lost its tense swagger. Her smirk turned into a wide-eyed grin.

With this mom in chief's protective, admonishing and encouraging gesture, a young woman transformed — at least for a moment. A student who had been putting on defensive airs became a graduate with an open smile — one that spoke of endless possibility rather than inevitable limits.

MYSTERY VISITOR

A student gets a glimpse of the special guest at Anacostia High School, then registers his surprise.

Photos by Bill O'Leary

WAGTIME

The Obamas keep a promise to Sasha and Malia when they accept a 6-month-old puppy from Sen. Edward M. Kennedy.

Photos by Bill O'Leary

TRAIL MIX OR TREAT?
Promoting healthy eating,
a Halloween-costumed
Michelle hands out dried
apricots, apples and papayas
with the M&M's and sugar
cookies to 2,600 kids and
parents. (Said a 9-year-old,
"I'm not a fan of dried fruit.")
The White House invited
children ages 5 to 14 from
11 area schools to file past
the front entrance of the
house, which was lit orange,
wrapped in cobwebs and
adorned with a giant black
spider with a dozen eyes.

Photo by Dayna Smith

PLANTING SEEDS

Helping fifth graders tend the White House Kitchen Garden in April may soften the first lady's image, but the larger message is nutrition.

Photos by Lois Raimondo

Photos by Marvin Joseph

66 *[By making a] small change in our family's diet and adding more fresh produce for my family, Barack, the girls, me, we all started to notice over a very short period of time that we felt much better.*"

Michelle Obama,
at a Kitchen Garden harvest

THAT'S ONE GIANT SWEET POTATO FOR MANKIND

October's Kitchen Garden harvest puts food on the table for the homeless as well as the White House.

Photos by Marvin Joseph

VEGGIE VISIT
Agriculture Secretary Tom Vilsack accompanies Michelle on a November visit to an elementary school in Fairfax County that has its own vegetable garden. Far right, the first lady helps open a new D.C. farmers market.

Above photos by Marvin Joseph

Photo by Dayna Smith

66 This isn't new anymore: people who've worked and struggled just like you; people who have defied the odds and defeated low expectations just like you; pioneers and trailblazers who have all challenged stereotypes and emerged as leaders just like I know all of you will."

Michelle Obama,
from her commencement address to Washington Mathematics Science Technology Public Charter High School graduates on June 3

Photo by Marvin Joseph

1 When a graduate makes a sassy gesture at the Washington Mathematics Science Technology commencement . . .

2 . . . Michelle Obama grasps the girl's hand and pulls it down to her chest . . .

3 . . . uses her other hand to hug the girl to her all the tighter . . .

4 . . . and changes a young graduate's smile, body language and commemorative moment.

ON, DASHER!
Michelle reads "The Night Before Christmas" to children at the National Christmas Tree lighting ceremony.

Photo by Ricky Carioti

5

Mrs. Ambassador

On the world stage, Michelle dashed and dazzled.
Russians were interested in her garden, Africans
in her heritage, while the English went into
a tizzy over this moment with the queen.

Photo by Daniel Hambury of Associated Press

SERVICE CALL: Addressing employees of the Corporation for National and Community Service, which oversees AmeriCorps and other service programs, in May at the Ronald Reagan Building.

Public silence and admiring curiosity were the dominant story lines for the first lady as she accompanied her husband on his first international trips as president. In Europe, she was the hugger in chief and the accessible fashion plate who held her own alongside France's glamorous first lady, Carla Bruni-Sarkozy — a former model. In Copenhagen, she was a sports fan and a hometown cheerleader as she led the Chicago 2016 delegation in an unsuccessful bid to host the Olympics. In Africa the mere sight of her had folks whipsawed by emotion as they saw past racial prejudices fade into a hopeful future.

During her foreign travels, she didn't represent the policies of the American government. That was for her husband to do. Instead, she symbolized the personality of the American people. She stood in for all of us. She was the ambassador of the popular culture we so ably export. She was a living symbol of the American dream. And we needed her to be gracious, confident and warm because that is how we would like the world to see us — at least most of the time.

Michelle made three official trips abroad during her first year in the White House. (She also made unofficial sojourns to both Paris and London with daughters Sasha and Malia during which she had no public schedule and spent most of her time

Photo by Nikki Kahn

sightseeing.) She was a woman of few wonkish words during her travels, disappointing some of her most ardent admirers who had hoped she would address topics ranging from the work-family tug of war to the historic nature of her position as an African American first lady.

Her most extensive and emotional remarks were delivered in October in Copenhagen standing before the International Olympic Committee. She made the case for sending the 2016 games to Chicago with stories about her late father, Fraser Robinson, who was stricken with multiple sclerosis. She described his love for sports, his fight against a debilitating disease and the encouragement he gave her and

her older brother, Craig Robinson — now a college basketball coach — to be brave, be bold and be confident.

A few poignant words marked her trip to London for April's G-20 meeting, and they resonated not because of the content, but because of their tenor. While visiting the Elizabeth Garrett Anderson girls school, her voice broke with emotion as she thanked the students — ethnic minorities from modest means — for their songs and dances: "You are precious and you touch my heart," she said. And the former child of Chicago's South Side proceeded to hug as many girls as would fit into her wide embrace.

While in London, Michelle hugged cancer patients and hospital volunteers, student singers and amateur actors, working women and other diplomatic spouses. By the time she visited Buckingham Palace, she had gone rogue with her embraces, setting off a diplomatic kerfuffle. During a small reception, the first lady reached out and hugged the British monarch. Protocol had been breached! The royal body touched! Breathless media analysis ensued over just how reckless a gesture it was to put a hand on the queen's back.

The official response from Buckingham Palace was: Stand down, people. The queen had made the first move, the palace declared. The first lady had merely reciprocated.

In early July, in little more than a week, the first couple, with Sasha and Malia in tow this time, mixed business with pleasure — racing to Moscow for a meeting at the Kremlin, then on to the Vatican for an audience with the Pope, and finally to Accra, Ghana, to tour a former fort where slaves were kept before beginning the horrors of the Middle Passage.

In the Russian capital, the locals had a single point of interest in the first lady. How does her garden grow? They admired her decision to plant the White House Kitchen Garden — the first significant veggie effort there since Eleanor Roosevelt's Victory Garden in 1943. And they respected her willingness to get dirty doing a bit of physical labor — at least for the cameras. It made her earthy and real, which was more important for Muscovites than her stylish wardrobe or outgoing personality. The garden also connected her to a Russian tradition — one closely associated with the Soviet era when so many families proudly and of necessity sowed vegetables in their own small plots. Michelle didn't have to say anything in Moscow. Her

FOREIGN DEBUT
Waiting while the president signs the guest book in April at Prague Castle in the Czech Republic.

White House photo by Pete Souza

carrots and potatoes did the talking.

In Italy, the first lady was a symbolic "spouse," married to a Group of Eight leader. The heads of state had gathered in L'Aquila, site of a devastating earthquake earlier in the year. In the ruined medieval city, Michelle was almost always part of an elegantly attired tour group that moved mutely from luncheon to museum to motorcade to dinner. The Italian whirlwind was solely about moments and images and propaganda. All too often, the symbolism failed to deliver much of an emotional wallop. It was particularly unsuccessful when the spouses toured one of the areas badly damaged by the earthquake. After a 10-minute walkabout, during which they spoke to no victims, they left for lunch.

But in Africa, things changed. Michelle was no more talkative there than she had been earlier in her trip. The details of her résumé were not well known and most people were ignorant of pet projects such as community service and aid to military families. But her presence had resonance. For the locals, here was a child of slavery, a distant cousin, perhaps, who'd made good. And they were anxious to meet her.

It didn't matter that the specifics of her family lineage remain uncertain or that Ghana ultimately may not even figure in it. Such fine details didn't matter to the people who came out hoping to catch a glimpse of her. All that mattered was that this African American woman had come triumphantly to Ghana, a country still recovering from the terrible scars of the slave trade. The president may have a Kenyan father, but unlike the first lady, he does not have a history of oppression embedded in his DNA. If the president, a black man who rose up out of a post-civil rights America, served

UH OH

The president steps on her dress at one of the inaugural balls.

Photo by Richard A. Lipski

as an emblem of future possibilities, then the first lady symbolized how much a painful history had been overcome. For many residents, she was the embodiment of optimism — proof that the past is not destiny.

In the early planning of her trip to Ghana, the first lady had been scheduled to visit the maternity ward in Accra's La General Hospital without her husband. The sight of this African American first lady — with her background in hospital bureaucracy, city government and community outreach — striding into a maternity ward filled with black African mothers-to-be would speak to the important role women play in building strong communities, sound economies and stable governments. But then the president decided to come along. With him by her side, would the message of the visit shift? Would it become a tableau that pointed to the role of government in caring for its people? No less important a point, just . . . different.

But as the first couple toured the hospital, the first lady held the hand of the nurse who led the way. "We are in this together," the gesture seemed to say.

In the neighborhood surrounding the hospital, the women were shopkeepers, students, errand runners and nurturers. They may spend their days trekking along dirt roads instead of dashing from one side of town to the other on a subway or in a minivan, but they too wrestle with balancing work and family. Women here related to her not as a distant figure in designer clothes or a yuppie gardener. They saw themselves in her — in both her physical attributes and in her independence.

When it came time for the Obamas to depart Accra, after less than 24 hours on the ground, a thousand guests — from dignitaries to Peace Corps

GHANA CEREMONY

Michelle's presence had a special resonance in Ghana, a country deeply affected by the slave trade.

Photo by Marvin Joseph

volunteers — crowded onto the tarmac at Kotoka International Airport. There was a military band in red dress uniform with tubas oompahing. Then came dancers spinning and high-stepping as their loose-fitting costumes caught the breeze and soared. It was a farewell for the first lady as much as for the first executive.

President Obama thanked everyone as his wife stood off to the side with Malia and Sasha. But when it came time for those last handshakes along the rope lines, it was the first lady who lingered.

She brought up the rear, her head barely visible above the crowd. Her husband slowed to wait for her. She wore a wide smile — as history caught up with the future.

HALLS OF CONGRESS
Michelle hugs an eighth grader from South Carolina in February at the joint session on the economy. At left, she is applauded in September at the joint session on health care reform.

Photos by Melina Mara

GETTING TO KNOW THEM
The Obamas and Bidens greet thousands in Baltimore the weekend before the inauguration.

Photo by Marvin Joseph

WASHINGTON BUSTLE

Clockwise from left, Vice President Biden, the president and the first lady join in the tribute to Sen. Edward M. Kennedy in March at the Kennedy Center; Sen. Patrick Leahy escorts the first lady to a reception for Supreme Court Justice Sonia Sotomayor; Michelle with Jill Biden and Alma Powell on Veterans Day at George Washington University.

Left photo by Katherine Frey, top and above by Marvin Joseph

MICHELLE OBAMA
HER FIRST YEAR AS FIRST LADY

SIGNING CEREMONY

Michelle showed up at a local school to watch her husband sign the Edward M. Kennedy Serve America Act.

Photo by Bill O'Leary

AFRICA UPDATE
Ghanaian women incorporated Obama's image into their traditional dress for the dances they performed after the U.S. president addressed parliament. The Obamas' visit brought an emotional response from the West African country.

Photos by Marvin Joseph

GETTING DOWN WITH THE SPEAKER
With House Speaker Nancy Pelosi, Michelle enjoys a performance by students from an Atlanta school.

Photo by Lois Raimondo

DOWN TO BUSINESS
A May briefing with her staff includes Jocelyn Frye, her policy director, above, and senior aide Trooper Sanders.

Photos by Melina Mara

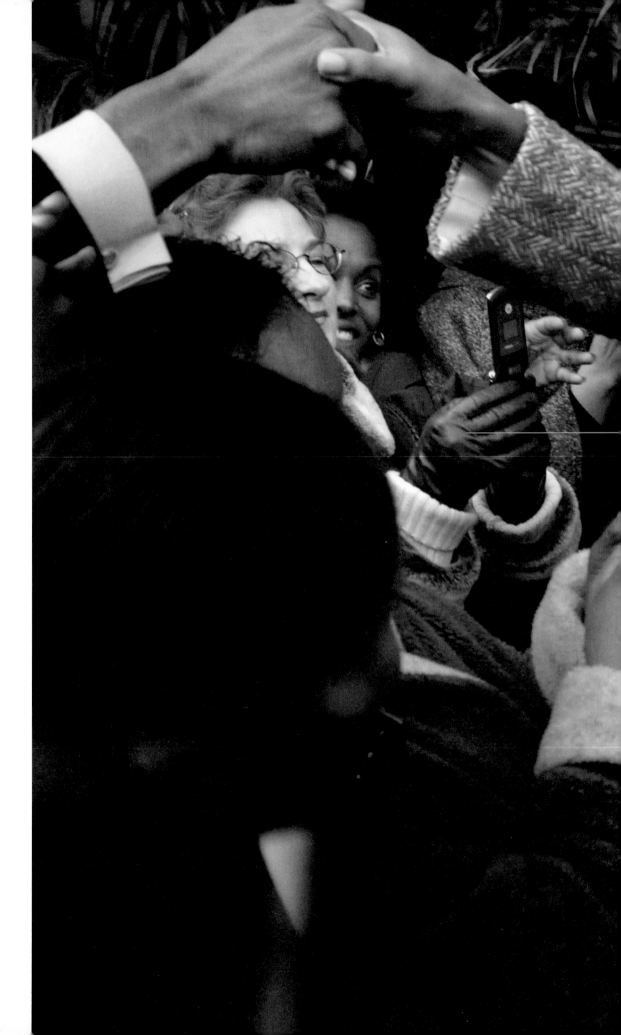

D.C. WELCOME

During her first week in Washington, Michelle is swamped after lunch with the mayor in a local restaurant.

Photo by Gerald Martineau

FORT HOOD TRAGEDY
The president and first lady
attend the Texas memorial
ceremony for the troops killed
in a massacre there.

Photos by Melina Mara

HAPPY COUPLE
At an inaugural ball — before the stimulus, the health care battle, the double-digit unemployment figures — the president and first lady are still savoring the moment.

Photo by Richard A. Lipski